TORAH QUEEN

Created and Written by Romoulous Malachi

Illustrations www.creative-illustrators.com
Sketches, Designs and Line Art by Jaira Jaro
Colorists: Norjie Aleta
Production Lead and Compiled by:
                    Mary Monette Barbaso

Published by MIROGLYPHICS
Library of Congress, Washington, D.C
Philadelphia, PA U.S.A.

YO! THAT WAS CRAZY! HOW DID YOU JUST DO THAT? ARE YOU SOME KIND OF MAGICIAN?

NO, BUT YOU ARE ABOUT TO WISH THIS WAS AN ILLUSION.

TRUST AND BELIEVE IS NOT GOING TO WORK THIS TIME.

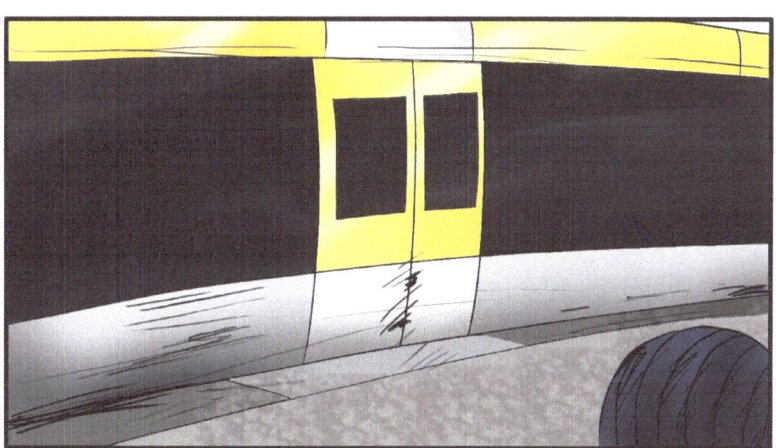

DING!!!

PUT DOWN YOUR WEAPONS AND LEAVE WHILE YOU HAVE THE CHANCE.

YOU HAVE TO LOVE THIS CITY. JUST WHEN YOU THINK, THAT YOU WITNESS SEEING EVERY WEIRDO. ANOTHER BEGINS TO SURFACE.

SHE USES HER ELECTRIC MAGNETIC FORCE TO SNATCH THE WEAPONS OUT OF THE PREDATOR HANDS. AISHA LEAPS BACK TO THE OTHER SIDE OF THE TRAIN AND THE TWO NEW YORK CITY VIGILANTES JOINS SHELIA, ADITYA, AND JADE FOX. THE FIVE PREDATOR ARE IN A STATE OF SHOCK AFTER WITNESSING THE SPECIAL POWERS OF PAMELA.

YO! LET'S JUST SQUASH THIS.

NO WE ARE NOT GOING TO SQUASH THIS. WE WANT TO PLAY THESE NICE TOYS YOU FELLAS GAVE US.

YOU LADIES ARE NOT PLAYING FAIR.

HE IS RIGHT. WE REALLY WASN'T GOING TO KILL YOU?

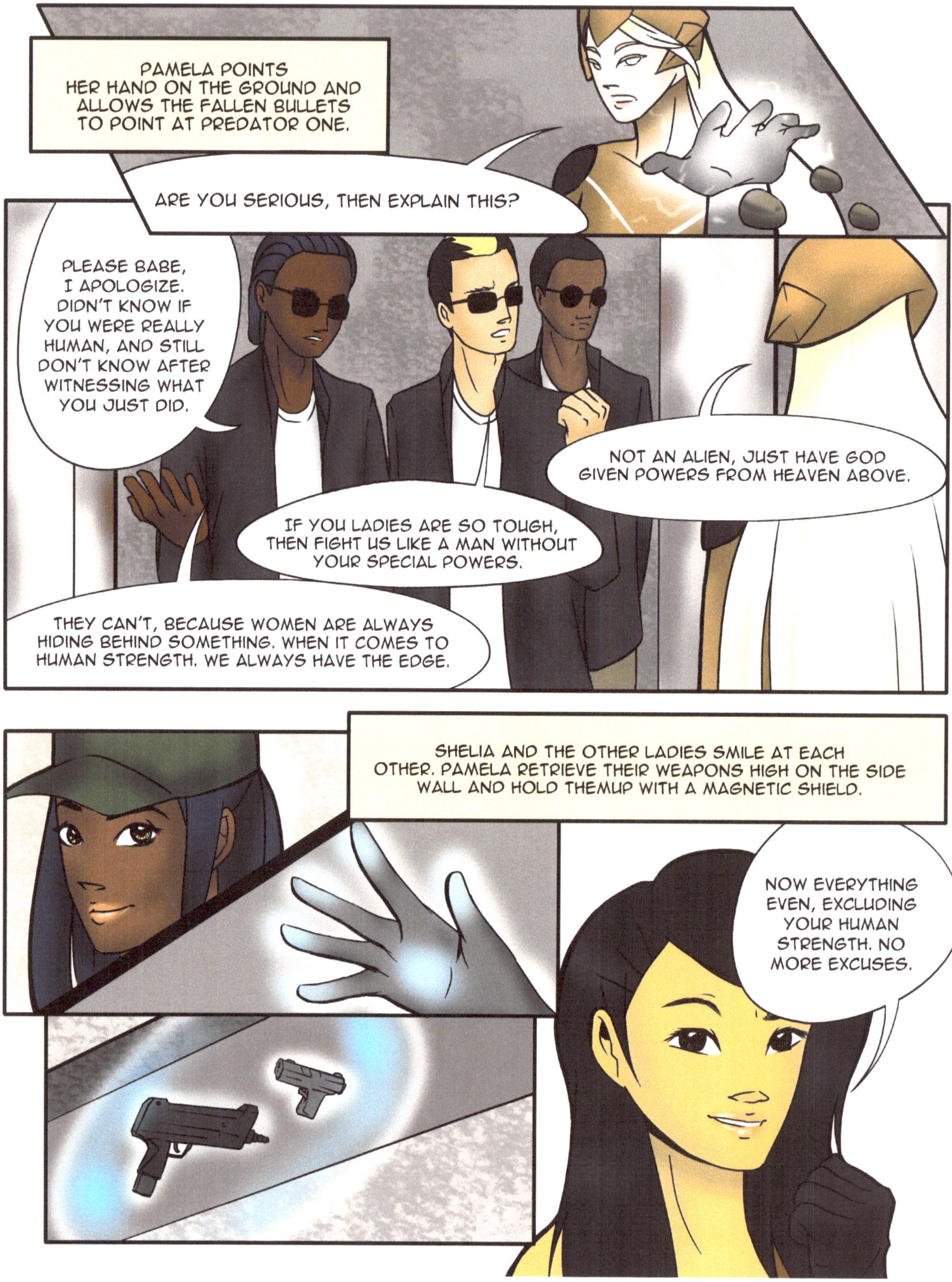

PAMELA POINTS HER HAND ON THE GROUND AND ALLOWS THE FALLEN BULLETS TO POINT AT PREDATOR ONE.

ARE YOU SERIOUS, THEN EXPLAIN THIS?

PLEASE BABE, I APOLOGIZE. DIDN'T KNOW IF YOU WERE REALLY HUMAN, AND STILL DON'T KNOW AFTER WITNESSING WHAT YOU JUST DID.

NOT AN ALIEN, JUST HAVE GOD GIVEN POWERS FROM HEAVEN ABOVE.

IF YOU LADIES ARE SO TOUGH, THEN FIGHT US LIKE A MAN WITHOUT YOUR SPECIAL POWERS.

THEY CAN'T, BECAUSE WOMEN ARE ALWAYS HIDING BEHIND SOMETHING. WHEN IT COMES TO HUMAN STRENGTH. WE ALWAYS HAVE THE EDGE.

SHELIA AND THE OTHER LADIES SMILE AT EACH OTHER. PAMELA RETRIEVE THEIR WEAPONS HIGH ON THE SIDE WALL AND HOLD THEMUP WITH A MAGNETIC SHIELD.

NOW EVERYTHING EVEN, EXCLUDING YOUR HUMAN STRENGTH. NO MORE EXCUSES.

I WANT CASPER THE FRIENDLY GHOST. SHE IS MAKE BELIEVE, BUT VERY SOON SHE WILL BECOME REALITY.

I WANT SISTER NINJA. I AM GOING TO SEND HER TO HELL, SO SHE CAN DANCE WITH THE DEVIL.

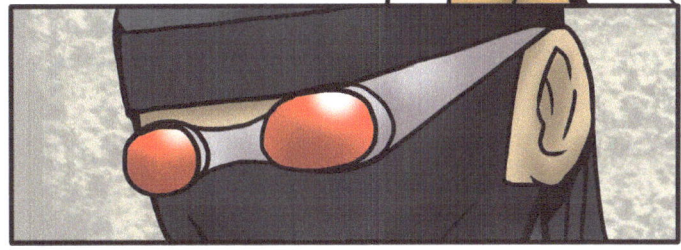

READY TO PLAY, BUT UNFORTUNATELY I DON'T FIGHT FAIR.

SOUNDS GOOD, AND NEITHER DO I.

LET'S PLAY.

I THOUGHT YOU WOULD NEVER ASK. YOU ARE A LONG WAY FROM CHINA TOWN.

WHERE WOULD YOU LIKE FOR ME TO SEND YOUR REMAINS?

THAT IS NOT YOUR CALL. GOD CONTROLS MY DESTINY NOT A WEAK PATHETIC MAN LIKE YOURSELF.

WE WILL SEE ABOUT THAT.

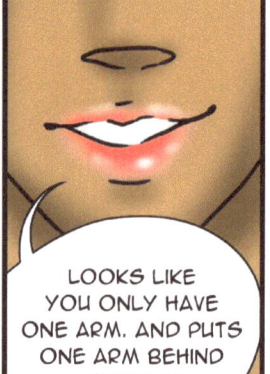

ADITYA FALLS TO THE GROUND AND THRUST HER LEG UP IN THE AIR TO KICK THE GROWN AREA WHILE LAYING ON HER BACK.

I TOLD YOU,
THAT I DON'T
FIGHT FAIR.

LOOKS LIKE YOU SHOULD HAVE STAYED HOME AND PRACTICE USING YOUR TOYS. BECAUSE YOU DEFINITELY DIDN'T KNOW HOW TO WORK IT.

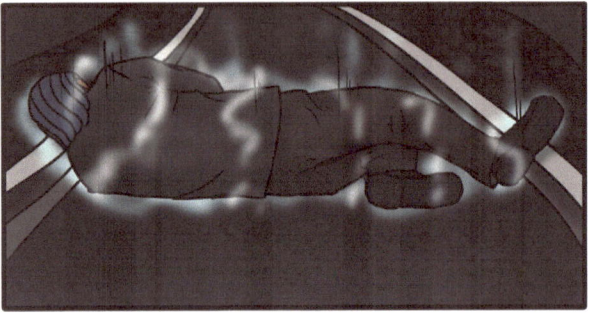

I THOUGHT WE AGREED TO FIGHT FAIR?

I GUESS YOU FORGOT, I AM A WOMAN. WE HAVE THE TENDENCY TO SWITCH UP ON YOU SOMETIMES.

PLEASE RELEASE ME, I WILL CHANGE FROM EVIL AND WICKED WAY. PLEASE DON'T LET THAT A-TRAIN CRUSH ME.

DON'T WORRY. I WON'T LET THAT TRAIN CRUSH AND KILL YOU.

YOU PROMISE.

YOU HAVE MY WORD. I WILL NOT LET THAT TRAIN CRUSH AND KILL YOU.

THE TRAIN IS CONTINUES TO APPROACH AND THE SOUND CAUSES THE PREDATOR TO GO INTO A STATE OF PANIC.

WHAT HELL ARE WE WAITING FOR?

PAMELA POINTS HER HAND AT THE ELECTRIC SHIELD THAT BURNS AND DISINTEGRATE HIS BODY FROM THE TRACKS. THE TRAINS CONTINUES TO APPROACH AND CROSSES OVER THE REMAIN OF ASHES.

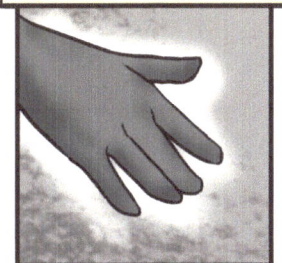

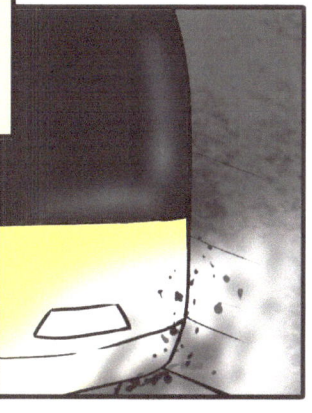

I TOLD YOU, THAT I WOULD KEEP MY PROMISE. I DID NOT LET THAT TRAIN CRUSH AND KILL YOU.

READY TO DANCE WITH THE DEVIL.

I DON'T DANCE WITH THE DEVIL.

THE LADIES OBSERVE THE REMAINS OF THE DECEASE PREDATORS.

PAMELA AND AISHA APPROACHES THE THREE FEMALE WARRIORS.

YOU LADIES ARE MEMBERS OF THE ELITE TORAH KNIGHTS WARRIORS.

YES WE ARE. SUJU AND THE DYNAMIC TRIO OFFERS YOU LADIES, AN INVITATION TO JOIN THE TORAH KNIGHTS.

SOUNDS GOOD, I THOUGHT YOU WOULD NEVER ASK.

LET'S GO LADIES, DESTINY AWAIT US.

THE NEW RECRUITS ENTER THE BATTLE SHIP AND EGYPT TAKES THEM TO NEXT DESTINATION PHILADELPHIA.

OUR NEXT STOP IS PHILADELPHIA, AND OUR SATELLITES HAVE DETECTED KARKASE ACTIVITY INSIDE CENTER CITY. THE PHOTOS THAT WE GATHERED DISPLAYED SEVERAL KARKASE SOLDIERS AND CYNIC WARRIORS THAT HAVE SURFACED IN SEVERAL AREAS INSIDE CENTER CITY. WE HAVE ALSO DETECTED SEVERAL SECTURIANS WARRIORS THAT ARE ALSO AFFILIATED IN THIS SECRET ATTACK.

WHAT IS OUR PLAN OF ACTION?

TO PROTECT AND DEFEND THE WORLD AGAINST TERRORISM.

SOUNDS GOOD TO ME.

THE SECTURIANS ARE HAVING A MEETING WITH KARKASE ABOUT DESTROYING A FEW NATIONAL MONUMENTS IN PHILADELPHIA. ECSTASY APPEARS ON THE BIG SCREEN WHILE FATALITY AND PETRA ARE PRESENT DURING THE SECRET MEETING WITH THE SECTURIANS.

YOUR MISSION IS TO CAUSE A DIVERSION IN PHILADELPHIA AND DESTROY A FEW OF THEIR NATIONAL MONUMENTS WHILE ANACONDA AND I SECRETLY STEAL RUSSIAN DOCUMENTS; WITH CLASSIFIED INFORMATION ON CREATING WEAPONS OF MASS DESTRUCTION.

NO WORRIES ECSTASY, THE TORAH KNIGHTS WILL NOT KNOW WHAT HIT PHILADELPHIA UNTIL IT IS ALL OVER.

SOUNDS GOOD FATALITY, WE WILL KEEP DISTRACTING THE KATALAMBANO UNTIL YOU ACCOMPLISH THE MISSION.

FATALITY ORDERS THE SECTURIANS TO CARRY OUT THE MISSION.

SECTURIANS, YOUR MISSION IS TO CAUSE A DIVERSION IN CENTER CITY WHILE KARKASE GOES ON A TOP SECRET MISSION IN EUROPE.

MOVE OUT!

THE SECTURIANSSECRETLY PLACE EXPLOSIVE DEVICES AROUND NATIONAL MONUMENTS AND FEDERAL BANKS THROUGHOUT THE CITY. SHELIA ISSUES OUT BLACK TACTICAL GEAR TO HER CREW AND THE TRAPAZONIANS. SHELIA HANDS OUT A UNIFORM TO AISHA, BUT SHE DOES NOT COMPLY.

HERE IS YOUR UNIFORM AISHA.

NO, THANKS. I ALREADY HAVE ONE.

EXCUSE ME AISHA, WE WORK AS TEAM AND THERE MUST BE UNIFORMITY.

NO DISRESPECT, BUT I AM ALREADY DRESSED IN BLACK TACTICAL GEAR. THE LAST TIME I CHECKED. I JOINED AN ELITE MILITIA NOT THE MILITARY.

VERY WELL AISHA, YOU HAVE POINT. I WILL RESPECT YOUR NINJA CODE. BUT MAKE NO MISTAKES.

THE ONLY MISTAKE THAT WAS MADE, IS WHEN THE SECTURIANS DECIDED TO INVADE OUR TERRITORY.

I KNOW THAT'S RIGHT!

THE TRAPAZONIANS EXIT THE BATTLE SHIP, WHILE THE TWO COPILOTS REMAIN BEHIND TO MONITOR THE SCREEN AND ENSURE THAT COMMUNICATION REMAIN STRONG BETWEEN THE WARRIORS.

THERE ARE SEVERAL KARKASE SOLDIERS AND CYNIC WARRIORS CAUSING CHAOS THROUGHOUT THE CITY AGAINST INNOCENT BYSTANDERS.

SHELIA DIRECTS SHAWNTAY, DEBORAH, TONYA, AND STEPHANIE TO CLOSE IN ON THE TERRORISTS.

THERE ARE SEVERAL KARKASE SOLDIERS THAT ARE TERRORIZING LOCAL RESIDENTS OF THE CITY. SHAWNTAY, TONYA, DEBORAH AND STEPHANIE APPROACH THE TERRORIST.

YOU KNOW WHAT THEY SAY ABOUT MEN THAT PREY ON THE WEAK.

SO TELL ME, WHAT DO THEY SAY?

MOST MEN THAT PRAY ON THE WEAK, DO IT BECAUSE THEY ARE SPINELESS COWARDS.

THAT'S RIGHT! YOU HAVE NO BACKBONE. JELLYBACK!

YOU WOMEN HAVE BIG MOUTHS AND YOU TALK TOO MUCH.

DON'T WORRY ABOUT KEEPING YOUR MOUTH SHUT, BECAUSE WE ARE ABOUT TO CLOSE IT FOR YOU.

ANOTHER KARKASE SOLDIER CHARGES AT SHAWNTAY, SHE DEMONSTRATES HER SKILLS WITH HER STICK AND ANNIHILATE THE TERRORIST. THE REMAINING FOUR ARE FIGHTING AGAINST THE OTHER THREE. DEBORAH IS CORNERED BY TWO SOLDIERS.

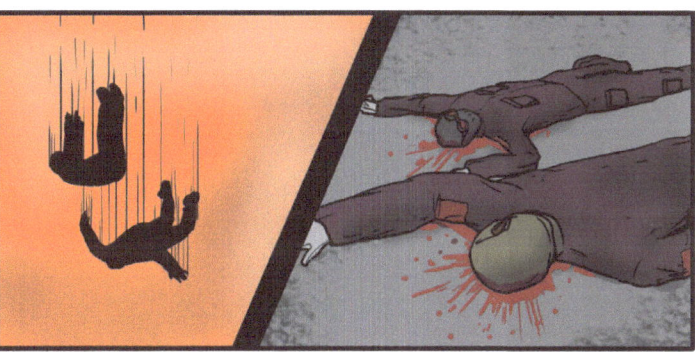

TONYA AND STEPHANIE ARE BEING APPROACHED BY THE LAST TWO KARKASE SOLDIER.

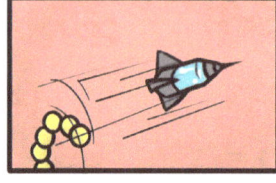

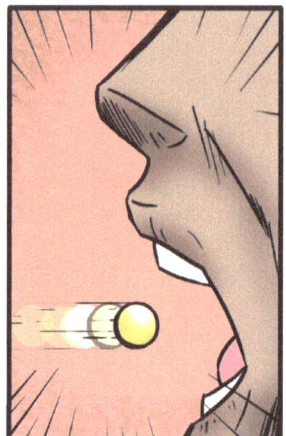

SHANWNTAY WALKS OVER ONE TO THE KARKASE SOLDIER WITH THE MELTED MASK OVER HIS REMAINS.

DIDN'T YOUR MOTHER TELL YOU, ABOUT BIG MOUTH WOMEN? YOU CAN NEVER MAKE THEM SHUT UP.

COMMANDER SHEILA, ALL KARKASE SOLDIERS ARE DOWN. NO SURVIVORS FOUND. MISSION ACCOMPLISHED.

OUTSTANDING RETURN WITH THE REST OF YOUR TEAM BACK TO THE BATTLESHIP. WE WILL FINISH OFF THE REST.

WON'T YOU NEED BACK UP AT THE U.S. MINT?

THANKS FOR THE GESTURE SHAWNTAY, BUT THAT COUNTERPART IS ALREADY IN EFFECT.

SHELIA, JADE FOX, AND ADITYA ARE ON THE SCENE WAITING FOR THE NEXT COUNTERATTACK FROM KARKASE. THERE ARE SEVERAL CYNIC WARRIORS SURROUNDING THE U.S. MINT BUILDING ALONG WITH FOUR SECTURIANS ABENA, BREATHE TAKER, MARJANI AND IMANI. FATALITY HAS ASSIGNED ABENA TO COMMAND THIS MISSION.

SECTURIANS OUR MISSIONS IS TO BREACH THE PERIMETER, DISARM ALL ALARM SYSTEMS INSIDE THE U.S MINT, AND STEAL AS MUCH US CURRENCY THAT WE CAN FOR THE NEXT FOUR HOURS. ONCE ALL SYSTEMS HAS BEEN ALARMED, THEN THE REST OF THE CYNIC WARRIORS WILL FOLLOW.

WE ARE GOING TO MAKE A FORTUNE FROM THIS.

FATALITY OVER HEAR THE SECTURIANS DISCUSSING POTENTIAL BENEFITS FROM STEALING US CURRENCY.

DO NOT ABORT THE MISSION WITH GREED, AND REMEMBER THIS CURRENCY PROVIDES FUNDING FOR RESEARCHING AND DESIGNING WEAPONS OF MASS DESTRUCTION TO RULE WORLD. NOW STOP TALKING AND FINISH THE MISSION.

OH REALLY FATALITY, HOW WOULD KNOW YOU OR KARKASE KNOW IF WE TOOK A FEW HUNDRED THOUSAND?

EACH SECTURIAN AND CYNIC WARRIOR WAS INJECTED WITH AN ELECTRONIC CHIP AND STEEL BRACELET WITH DEVICE TO DISPLAY A HOLOGRAM. EACH TERRORIST ASSIGNED TO MISSION RIGHT ARM STARTS GLOWING AND CAN VISUALLY SEE AN IMAGE OF ECSTASY ON DISPLAY. EXCEPT FOR BREATH TAKER.

DOES THIS ANSWER YOUR QUESTION ABENA? YOU SECTURIANS ARE STARTING TO BE A DISAPPOINTMENT. RESPECT YOUR AUTHORITY, AND I WILL EXPECT NOTHING BUT ABSOLUTE INTEGRITY DURING THIS MISSION. I WILL INVESTIGATE AND EVALUATE EVERY MOVE YOU MAKE. THEN IF FOUND GUILTY MY LOYAL AND FAITHFUL WARRIOR BREATH TAKER WILL LIVE UP TO HIS NAME.

BREATHE TAKER CLINCH FLASHES AND INFERRED LIGHT ON A CYNIC WARRIOR THEN THE SECTURIANS WITNESS THE CYNIC WARRIOR'S BODY VAPORIZES, AFTER CLINCHING HIS FIST.

THAT IS YOUR FIRST AND LAST WARNING. JUST ONE MORE NOTE, IF ANYTHING HAPPENS TO BREATHE TAKER. I AND FATALITY WILL BE HIS BACK UP. DO NOT ABORT THE MISSION, AND KEEP IT MOVING.

ABENA, YOU HAVE A BIG MOUTH. IF YOU CONTINUE TO KEEP TALKING, THEN I WILL HAVE TO CLOSE IT FOR YOU.

BREATHE TAKER SHINES AND INFERRED LIGHT ON HIS CHEST.

DO I MAKE MYSELF CLEAR?

ABSOLUTELY!

THE SECTURIANS ENTER THE U.S. MINT BUILDING AND USE EXTREME PRECAUTION WHEN DISARMING ALL ALARMS INSIDE THE NATIONAL MONUMENT. THERE ARE TEN CYNIC WARRIORS REMAINING OUTSIDE THE BUILDING AND SIMULTANEOUSLY GUARDING THE PERIMETER. THE SECTURIANS CLIMB TO THE TOP OF THE U.S. MINT'S ROOF AND EACH TERRORIST PULL OUT A LASER CUTTER.

THE LASER ELECTRONIC DEVICES LIGHTS UP AND BURNS A FOUR HOLES WITH A DIAMETER OF FIVE FEET IN WIDTH.

THEN INSTANTLY VAPORIZES THE CONCRETE, METAL, AND OTHER ELEMENTS USED TO CREATE THE FOUNDATION OF THE ROOF.

THE SECTURIANS INJECT A METAL STAKE ON THE SIDE OF EACH HOLE. THEN HOOK 300 FEET OF CORD TO THAT WILL ALLOW THEMSELVES TO REPEL DOWN INSIDE THE MAIN ENTRANCE OF THE U.S. MINT.

THE SECTURIANS BEGIN DISARMING THE ALARM SYSTEMS, SUDDENLY EACH SECTURIANS WITNESS A RED LASER POINTED AT THE CENTER OF THEIR CHEST.

THERE FOUR TRAPAZONIANS THAT HAS THEM SURROUNDED. EBONY FROM ORIGINS DETROIT, JESSICA IS FROM CHICAGO, MONICA ORIGINS LAS VEGAS, AND VICTORIA ORIGINS LOS ANGELES. VICTORIA IS HAS BEEN ASSIGNED AS THE DESIGNATED LEADER AND CALLS OUT THE TERRORIST.

DROP YOUR WEAPONS AND SURRENDER AT ONCE, OR THE TRAPAZONIANS WILL NOT TAKE ANY PRISONERS.

FATALITY AND ECSTASY ARE OBSERVING THE SCENE. ECSTASY BRIEFLY COMMUNICATES WITH FATALITY.

FATALITY, PUT OUT THE WELCOME FOR THESE NEW VIGILANTES. LET'S SHOW THEM WHAT HAPPENS WHEN YOU START A WAR WITH KARKASE. INITIATE OPERATION MEGABLAST.

FATALITY DELIVERS A MESSAGE TO THE FOUR CORNED SECTURIANS.

IGNITE OPERATION MEGABLAST.

THE FOUR SECTURIAN SIMULTANEOUSLY SPIT OUT A PILL ON THE GROUND THAT CREATE SMOKE BOMB AND VANISHES FROM THE SCENE.

WHILE QUICKLY HOISTING THEMSELVES TO THE TOP OF ROOF WITH THE ELECTRONIC CORDS. AFTER THE SMOKE CLEARS THE FOUR TRAPAZONIANS SEE THE CABLES HANGING FROM TOP OF THE CEILING WITH HOLES ON THE ROOF, WHILE DANGLING IN THE AIR.

SHELIA WE WILL MOVE OUTSIDE THE U.S. MINT. THE SECTURIANS HAS MADE AN ESCAPE.

SHELIA, JADE FOX, AND ADITYA WITNESS FOUR TERRORIST FLEEING FROM THE BUILDING ALONG WITH THE CYNIC WARRIORS. THE THREE FEMALE COMMANDERS BEGIN FIRING ROUNDS AT THE SECTURIANS AND THE CYNIC WARRIORS.

THE TERRORIST RETURN FIRE AND BEGIN CHARGING AT THEM WITH FULL FORCE. THE FOUR TRAPAZONIANS FLANKS THE TERRORIST FROM A BLIND SPOT ON THE RIGHT AND KILLS TWO CYNIC WARRIORS. THE TERRORIST SCATTER IN DIFFERENT DIRECTIONS AND TAKE COVER.

ABENA HAS VISUAL ON JADE FOX AND MANAGES TO SUPPRESS ENOUGH FIRE TO MOVE IN ON JADE FOX. ABENA IS NOW TEN FEET AWAY FROM HER ADVERSARY AND WATCHES JADE FOX RELOAD HER SEMI-AUTOMATIC.

ABENA THROWS A LASER CHINESE STAR THAT DESTROYS THE BARREL OF HER WEAPON. THIS SUDDEN ATTACK SURPRISES JADE FOX, AND SHE REACHES HER BACK UP WEAPON. ABENA HAS CLOSED IN ON HER.

LOOKS LIKE YOU ARE A LONG WAY FROM CHINA TOWN.

WHY DOES EVERYONE KEEPS REMINDING ME OF THAT?

YOU JUST DON'T HOW BAD, THAT I HAVE BEEN WAITING FOR THIS DAY. I FINALLY GET TO ASSASSINATE OF THE WORLD MOST DANGEROUS VIGILANTES.

CORRECT. HIRED ASSASSIN.

WHATEVER! YOU ARE NOT ON THE GOVERNMENT PAY ROLL. IF ANYTHING YOU ARE WANTED JUST LIKE US, EXCEPT YOU DECIDED TO TAKE MATTERS INTO YOUR OWN HANDS.

IT'S A DIRTY JOB, BUT SOMEONE HAS TO DO IT.

THE ONLY THING DIRT ABOUT THIS SCENARIO IS YOU BEING BURIED UNDERNEATH IT.

JADE FOX AND ABENA BEGIN TO BATTLE.

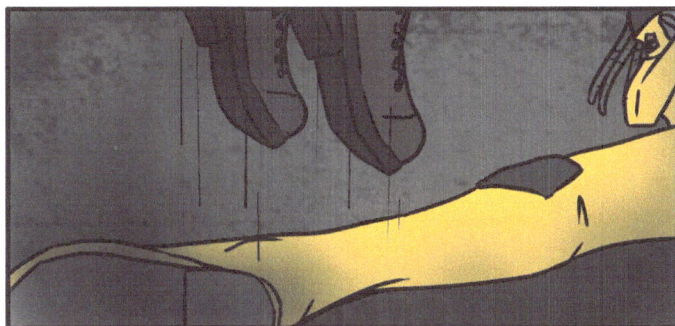

THERE HAS BEEN A CHANGE OF PLANS. THIS IS TOO MUCH LIKE WORK FOR ME. IT WAS NICE MEETING YOU.

THEN SUDDENLY ABENA BENDS BACKWARD JUST BEFORE THE ARROW PENETRATES HER CHEST.

SHE RECOGNIZES PHILADELPHIA'S VIGILANTES LAUREN AND LATOYA. SHE QUICKLY LEAVES THE SCENES AND REGROUP WITH THE OTHER TERRORIST.

WHILES ABENA RUNS FOR SAFETY. THE REMAINING CYNIC WARRIORS CONTINUE TO BATTLE AGAINST THE QUADROZOIDZ.

LAUREN ASSASSINATES THREE CYNIC WARRIORS IN A ROW. LATOYA ASSASSINATED TWO. VICTORIA KILLS TWO MORE CYNIC WARRIORS. THE FOUR SECTURIANS AND THE ONE REMAINING CYNIC WARRIOR TAKE COVER.

BREATHE TAKER PULLS OVER AN ELECTRONIC DEVICE AND CREATE AN ELECTRONIC SHIELD.

FATALITY AND HER FLIGHT TEAM NAVIGATE TO THE ELECTRONIC DEVICE THAT ALSO OPERATES AS TRACKING SYSTEM. THEN THE BATTLE SHIP HOVERS OVER THE DEVICE AND SUCTION IT UP INSIDE CHAMBERS OF THE CONTROL ROOM.

THEN CLOSES THE HATCH AND VANISHES IN THIN AIR.

THE TRAPAZONIANS WALKS OVER TO THE SAME LOCATION WHERE THE SECTURIANS.

IT LOOKS LIKE THE SECTURIANS WERE TWO STEPS AHEAD.

MAYBE SO, BUT THEIR MISSION HAS BEEN ABORTED. THAT IS ALL THAT MATTERS TO ME.

THE TRAPAZONIANS RETURN TO THE BATTLESHIP FOR THEIR AFTER ACTION REVIEW.

SUJU AND THE DYNAMIC TRIO APPEARS ON THE SCREEN.

EXCELLENT WORK WARRIORS. YOU SAVED THE CITY OF PHILADELPHIA FROM A SECRET TERRORIST ATTACK. YOUR REACTION WAS IMPRESSIVE TO THIS SPONTANEOUS COUNTERATTACK AGAINST KARKASE AND THE SECTURIAN.

TRAPAZONAINS REMAIN VICTORIOUS, AND THEY CAME TO FIGHT.

ADITYA SMILES AND SPEAK SOFTLY TO HERSELF. AND SEE AN IMAGE OF HER FATHER IN THE BACK OF HER MIND.

FIRST IT WAS ONLY KARKASE WE HAD TO BATTLE AGAINST. NOW IT'S THE SECUTURIANS, AND QUESTION IS? WHO WILL EVOLVE AFTER THEM?

DO NOT FOCUS ALWAYS TRYING TO SOLVE A MYSTERY. IT IS IMPERATIVE THAT WE STAY IN FOCUS ON OUR MEANS OF SURVIVAL, AND WAIT FOR TIME REVEAL ITS ELEMENTS.

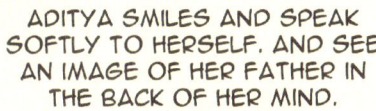

.

www.ingramcontent.com/pod-product-compliance
Lightning Source LLC
Chambersburg PA
CBHW060825290526
45792CB00005BB/1805